John Prine would have loved these poems. He'd have taken them on the road, wished he'd written them. Garrett Stack makes it look so easy: nothing fancy, and nothing should be. It won't take long to recognize what he has accomplished is anything but easy. Because of Stack's mastery of line, tone, movement, sound, timing, and voice, after just a few poems, you'll realize that you're not reading. You're listening, listening to distinct and captivating voices rich with surprise because each enters an environment that within the world of work is unexpected. This gang is worthy of your empathy. And as Prine sang, I bet you'll want to say, "Hello in there."

—Jack Ridl, author of *Practicing to Walk Like a Heron*
and *Saint Peter and the Goldfinch*

WORKING LIVES SERIES

BOTTOM DOG PRESS

YEOMAN'S WORK
POEMS

GARRETT STACK

WORKING LIVES SERIES
BOTTOM DOG PRESS
HURON, OHIO

Bottom Dog Press, Inc.
PO Box 425, Huron, OH 44839
Lsmithdog@aol.com
http://smithdocs.net

CREDITS:
General Editor: Larry Smith
Cover & Layout Design: Susanna Sharp-Schwacke
Cover Image: "Garage" by Rob Newbold (www.newbould.net)

ACKNOWLEDGMENTS

My gratitude to the editors from the following journals for generously agreeing to publish my work, albeit potentially in an altered form than seen in this volume.

2 Bridges Review: This is the one about going home, Where this poem belongs; *3288 Review*: Yeoman's work, Cleaning out the study, Some mornings; *American Journal of Poetry*: Fair; *Blueline*: The Changing Woman Moves West; *Blue Mountain Review*: Spectacles; *Connecticut River Review*: What the security guard won't say; *Foliate Oak*: Butterfly wrangling, Duggers, When I wake in a darkened room; *I-70 Review*: The Ballerina's Husband, A wish for my unborn child at Christmas; *The MacGuffin*: Spring Harana; *Naugatuck River Review*: Float; *Oakland Review*: The old professor, Transcontinental, At the Friday Skate; *PacificREVIEW*: Advice for a savage child; *Pine Row*: Stopping by the Quik-Fil before dawn; *Pinyon*: Selecting a Reader; *Southern Poetry Review*: Ernestine; *Voices*: The Heart Failure Fan Club.

Contents

3. River

For the women who shaped me.

Diurnal

He's got three boats and no motors
oil slick rainbow steel toes a knack
for calibrating torque wrenches
these things are often enough

            From the kitchen sink she watches
            her laundry flutter over a rusted Ford
            double checks the clabbering clouds
            fretting she's got it all hung out to dry

He loves to feel the biting
zipper peel skin from skin
after a day crawling round
the mouth of a big black Mack

            She'd prefer he changed
            out in the detached garage
            and left his black-stained
            day where it belongs

He pictures his daughter spinning
slowly like he never did
at their own quiet reception
in the First Lutheran basement

            She's had him in for fitting
            twice just for the flutter
            she gets seeing him tuxedoed
            the little thrill like feeling Jesus

He pays for lasers amps smoke
machines in the non-smoking
KC hall that costs just enough
to be exactly too much

            She sweats sewing the new skein
            of pistachio green taffeta just knowing
            he'll never get the grease off
            his hands in time for the wedding

He remembers her unhardened
hands and the sound from the simple
speaker as the British boys sang
Don't Let Me Down

            She only hopes the honeymoon
            bears no fruit and she returns
            honestly with picture after picture
            of nothing but open water

1. KITCHEN

Stopping by the Quik-Fil before dawn

for a coffee, darts,
a homemade sour
cream cruller. Sleet

got here too quick
this year, but the bed
stayed dry overnight,

and it'll be Jumbo's
for clubs at lunch;
so, there's that sorted.

Nodding at the self-
pour station, I ask
about the depths

of other men's
wells, wood stacks,
their maintenance

unnoticed as daily
prayer. And me?
I'm throwing up

a fresh new sign
on the old bank
near Ludington,

its third change
of hands in as many
years and funny

how they give you
just as much to create
as to destroy. It's cold

getting colder
but I've got chains
for my snow tires,

this sweetened
cup, high beams
for the lengthening dark.

When I wake in a darkened room

I want to go home
              and talk earnestly
              over split lips
to feel the old cold
              through the slats
and drink the night
              and the fire
with the boys
              grown fat
              not soft
waiting for their war
              their hands
              do the talking
and their wives
              these strangers
              who traded in aprons
              but not aches
and to remember
              just once more
what it's like
              to fall asleep
              here in the tall grass
with only ashes
              waiting for me
              to wake
and the sun
              streaming in
              through the slits
in my eyes

Fair

God knows you can't dig your way out
specially when all you got is axes
and lumber's not worth the gas. Spent

your life hunting and hunted across the state
line, the line of scrimmage, and maybe
you don't even want out when the sand

is your only option. Come home draped
in medals and metal and certainly ghosts
or maybe just the flag. Wind up painting

houses or trying a trade, but your old man
never got the hang of carburetors and who
the fuck is going to buy a handmade chair?

All you really want is a fair shake, one more
shot at that 4th and 3, that 12 pointer, the last
Saturday slow grind. You wake to children

playing at the bus stop like the yipping
of coyotes and your first thought is where's
my gun and your second thought is Jesus.

Shaving in the shower

To relearn the contours
of this stranger's face,
feel your way through
and avoid the dueling

cruelties of mirror and chilly
morning floor. As a rule
don't force reflection
until the razor's had a say

and to hell with missed
whiskers, their execution
stayed for one more day
they'll enjoy the breeze.

A warning: don't linger
overlong or the heater
will abandon you, but
hurry and pay in flesh

just like sex and fist fights,
it's about the timing
it's about blood and cold
water circling the drain.

Aubade, for my son

When you lie on my chest in defiance
of the bright morning window
and the pediatrician's directive,

we'll defect together to separate nation
states of the unconscious continent.
I'll retire to the petty shores

of forgotten math tests and abstract lust
while you return to the womb, to the bone
density shafts of sonogram shadow

inhabited only by the misty ghosts
alive behind your unfinished eyes.
And every morning we carry off

this round trip of impossible distance,
just another miracle orchestrated
by a gently rocking conspiracy of two.

Saw Me Six Ways

Seven a.m. my limbs
from the drying shed
and into the stove, these
fallen arms swapped
for fried eggs. Eight,
and it's off to the dewy
mill to cut out my heart-
wood and saw it to slabs.
Slender for the siding,
shingles, a new first step
on the old landing. Stout
for beam and board, even
now I've strength enough
to bear another story.
Lunch on my stump,
cold sandwiches, hot
coffee, but don't neglect
the water in the creek,
pure enough to merit
dolorous decades
rooting through stone.
And of my fallen crown,
leave my leaves
and tender finger
tendrils where they lie.
At dusk, the children
will gather to smile
and watch them burn.

Today I'm buying flowers for everyone

just because it's raining. In the grey half-
light I will ring florists from my couch
and lounge, as bouquets make their way
to my loved ones. First, flowers for my wife

for the obvious reasons; another for Mom
same reason, past tense. One for the mail
man for never failing to deliver the *Penny
Saver*. Six for my exes: the true heroes

of the story. A lovely arrangement
for Ms. Kissling for flunking me
in English because it's time to bury
that hatchet. One for the flight attendant

who gave me the whole can, and another
for the girl at the Gap for watching me try
on eight pairs of pants and never laughing.
Lilies for the night librarian who I believe

is in love with me; roses for the barista
who loves the idea of me. One bouquet for Pops
for sharing his cardiomyopathy—the card
will read *No hard feelings*—and one for my uncle

because every man should receive flowers
at least once. Finally, arrangements
for the florists who surprisingly get flowers
less often than everyone imagines. And for me,

nothing. I'll just lie here and listen to the rain
maybe catch a nap while blossoms blow
across the country and wait for the phone
to start ringing.

Some mornings

I torture the kettle
for strength,
just like cowboys

cooked it.
Boiling water
down the throat

of an old tin
pot, the loamy
grounds richer

for slow rain and all
that's missing
is fire. No prairie

coals here in
the yellow kitchen,
our forgotten embers

scattered now
as sleeping cattle
waiting for the sun.

Beloved at the Glass Onion Diner

Again, she has stayed
too long, her tip slipped
from the sideboard
into a widow's passing
apron. She won't ask
for a refill, filled as she is
with eggs, child.
She's tuned to empathy,
to the kitchen clunks
and *fucks*, but there is no fast
bread here, no little mercy
for the lean times
no pork bone stew
no bones in the backyard.
She'd like some blackberry pie,
sweet coffee for her too tired
teeth, but the waitresses'
unwelcoming eyes spill
their own hard sadnesses,
their empty bedrooms already full
of their own ghosts.
Her taxi is waiting, the driver
like all drivers is named
River, like all rivers
is equally ready to drown her
or carry her on.

What the security guard won't say

is that it's her birthday
and her husband held
a single candle singing
into their dark morning
bed. She won't bother you
about the six daily buses
or the heavy cost of her
light blue uniform. At 5'2"
on tiptoe and armed
(taser, frown) she orders
her narrow world with
whispers, *No pictures,*
please. Restrooms below.
The benches are not for her,
but you may sit and watch
the master of two rooms
orchestrate serenity. She
won't mention the sculptor
who came to destroy
his own ceramic babies
or the concealed scotch
tape on the towering West
Gallery installation and
she won't tell you how,
but with a single breath
she can make the whole thing
sway.

Following the apocalypse

You will be the first to go
because our new world won't ask
for poetry. Then the teachers
and Doers and DREAMERS

because they were mostly dead
already. Trade will remain steady
for zealots and timber men
while the one-eyed moon

shiners and dusty gun slingers
will catch their second wind.
The rest of us ticks will scuttle
back inside our shiny vinyl eggs

to wait for the earth, that dog,
to shake us from its drying
back. How long do you think
the power will be out before

the wolves return to howling
around our freshly darkened yards?
First imagine the huddling silence.
Now think how loud the birds will be.

Ernestene

She still writes letters on triple thick
stock with the only fountain pen
she's ever owned. Ninety-one and lashed

to her wheelchair like a sailor
to the mast, her script is fine
as the day she mastered the capital

Q. Her letters never reveal
that instead of finishing high school
she stayed home making breakfast

and supper for seventeen farmhands
and a strong-hearted husband twice
her age. She won't mention pie crust

and how they don't use hog fat
like they used to or how the crows
lined every wire in Worthington

when his lean black hearse rolled
heavily through town. Maybe
she'll mention the weather down

Daytona way, back pain, the state
of her rhododendrons. But I can still see
her sitting next to Beulah Ashford

in the one room schoolhouse, falling
in love with her own handwriting
as the fountain pen carves his name

Junior
Junior
Junior

Purgatory

At the wedding in the meadow,
we crowded the mountain's
netted silence. The old cream
clouds trailed through their blue
bowl to the tune of clapping
aspens and below she walked in
white as bright as lightning.
She stopped
      you cannot cage the rain
He smiled
      you cannot trap the sky
She took his hand
      but maybe you can hold it for a time

Stroke

The taxidermist's
skin now hangs
flat off one cheek
like an unfinished
job. He works
only the good arm
to greet the men
who crowd out
his caretakers,
who guilt-rub
their tight jaws
and clench their
still strong fists
and stare right
past the blinking
machines wondering
why him and how's
he gonna skate
again and just who
is gonna pay
for all of this?

Out of the blue

The messages came in grey
November, some stranger
plunking tidbits in my inbox
like nickels dropped
in the kitchen tin can
marked *Ice Cream Money*.
The usual fare at first:
bad jokes about good
women, priests in bars,
the Irish, of course.
Tom Maloney faithfully passed
on chain mail and schlock lists
(#7 will shock you.)

And then Martha
got sick, and the long-faced
horses ordering whiskey soured
into updates on chemo,
doctors' best guesses, vitals
reports for us loved ones.
I could have let him know
that he had the wrong guy,
that some cousin with a similar
address was sitting somewhere
in the dark.

But we waited
for the last dime
to drop and when it did
it fell softly as Martha did
while we slept. Along with hours
for the visitation, an attachment:
Eulogy_thoughts?
I click reply, stare until
the screen turns black.

Day-old news

when the trip to the mailbox
is the better part of a gravel mile
and the mailman in his European
pickup is in no particular hurry,
we let the news wait. Waking
to the sound of a braying mule
alters the precedence:
boil the coffee
        rack the hay
                gather the eggs
                        kindle the stove.
Wise we feel as we sit chatting
over yesterday's paper. Look
who's in trouble. Isn't that
sweet? What's another word
for *prance*—five letters?

Sure, they're yesterday's answers,
but right now, we're not hurrying.
We're going to hang the wash
out on the line, stack some wood
behind the barn, maybe check
if the watermelons have swollen
to ripe. Later we'll take the walk
past the goslings down by the pond,
cut through whipping tall grass
and collect our letters. Don't
open the paper, it'll keep
till morning—open some wine,
it's been another long day.

Girl, arguing loudly with Mike on her cell phone in the library

she's 19ish and nameless
but now you know Mike (prick)

drawn as you are
to breaks in the weather

you wonder about Mike
his macadam heart

did he answer the phone like
look out below

your eyelids will grow
heavy as they do before rain

you'll check out two books
and read neither

She collects the broken birds

There's need and there is
want, and a taut line between
that stretches west from her
and once a day tugs without
warning. You'll feel it hum.
It is too much. It is not a rope.
You cannot hang yourself
with it or tie yourself down
to waiting rusty railroad spikes.
It won't pull you clear
of the deep canyon's maw, but
it is not a tenuous thing.
Like braided suture silk
it binds and mending makes
new flesh to knit the fissures
and gashes scoring your ragged
wings. She collects the broken
birds in her soft hands, hollow
as clay cups and filled with extra
thread. She'll let you go,
lightly tethered and won't
need to reel you back in.

Selecting a Reader
—after Ted Kooser

First, I would have him be morning-ugly
and stumbling haphazardly upon my poetry
at the Formica table over eggs,
his cheeks still rubbed red raw
from wind. He should be wearing
a frown, a new one, dirty
from not having money enough for her tuition.
He will take out his kerchief, and there
in the kitchen, he will blow his nose
over my poems, then put the book back
upon her textbook stack. He will say to himself,
"For this kind of money, I could get
my tractor fixed." But he won't.

Wood thrush

Like the thrush
who keeps returning
to the unfilled fall feeder
and catches his own dark
eyed reflection
in the empty glass,
you keep looking
for yourself
in these poems

2. FIELD

Yeoman's work

When waking to water
rapping the shake roof,
it's easy to believe it's raining

everywhere on Earth.
Blame your father
for the hand-me-down

labor and inherited cold
of dawn in the clapboard
cabin. Blame the Virgin

for all the rain. The dream
is always the same, one kestrel
sitting on a fence post

speaking with your mother's
voice: *you can lay it all down.*
But sore at the world

is no way to wake. Raise
the sash, there's mist
on the field and rinse water

by the four post. Pull on
your wellies and stretch
out the stiff leg, if you hurry

you'll pace the rain
and the fence needs mending
before the late sun breaks.

Spring Harana

You get those days
you just start yearning
for a funeral. Maybe

it's the same thing
as sniffing for spring,
a chance to dust off

the suit and catch up
with old neighbors
and no one expects you

to dance. Instead
of starting the snow
blower, there is pork,

tasteful plastic table-
cloths, a young girl
in a new black dress

who moves like a brook trout
in the stained light
of the rectory basement

and who doesn't yet grasp
how all of this
winter business works.

Everybody loves an old red barn

Covered with vines or lichen, cow

blood and you never know if there's

trucks back there, maybe hand-built

highways close in and semis squash

cicadas or a chicken hawk crying

abandoned in the field. The farm is

for sale and you just can't help it

licked and paint stripped like dried

orchards or weed-choked Apache

wooden forts rusting away. Though

their drum brakes you can hear

over hunted hare, and sweet corn lies

dying or drying up but still

you want it, to paint it red all over again.

The gravediggers listen to "Jack and Diane"

The weather's turned toward
interment, and sun-softened
turf offers further mercies
for the diggers who open up

the earth and their shirtfronts
lifting their voices from the pit
out across the empty lawn.
They'd laugh if they could

see me jogging through, too
interloping on the hallowed,
hollow but for all these
bones. It could be beautiful

to lay down on the new grass
to quit singing our little ditties
and let life go on, apply for asylum
as refugees here among the resting.

Emeritus

He still rides his father's bike,
a Schwinn Collegiate II
in blue fading to mottle,

and mounted to the bars
a mesh detachable basket
ferries all the lamentable

précis, personal essays, self-
reflections which flutter
like koinobori windsocks

ahead of his steady sandaled
passing. Today the skirling
wind snatches some up

and flings *The Reasons*
I Chose Nursing and
A Passion for Public

Accounting over the cooling
quad where coeds or janitors
pluck them from choking

gutters and potted geraniums.
The old professor pedals on
as finches, robins, other late

nesters carry off *A Future*
Construction Manager's
Tale and all the rest

of the sifting aspirations
to insulate their small nests
against the closing season.

Spalted maple

For the bridal gift, I conceived a box:
a tabernacle for ticket stubs, receipts, the litter
of treasured memories. So I went to see my uncle
in the woods. The barn hasn't felt a hoof beat
in years, just beer cans and spiders and rain,
but the old equipment still runs fine and tended

well enough to keep rust off and your fingers
on. He shows me the belt sander-table saw-
jointer-planer-lathe, hulking pale green ogres
red stamped *General International* with Canadian
pride. But first we look at wood, and down
from the loft comes every plank and beam and board

he ever cut: cherry in red so soft it seems the pulp
is blushing, ash that feels made for morning
coffee and public radio, hornbeam—or iron wood
the locals say—great ruin of wrists and axes.
But one board's different, pale and spidered
with black map lines on white wood grain.

He says that like a good sailor it caught the rot,
and normally it's no good and damn tricky
to cut, but if you snag it at just the right time
and let it age properly the lumber's sound.
He called it wedding wood and winking said
she'll hold up better than most.

The Heart Failure Fan Club

meets informally around the polyvinyl
coffee table in waiting room B where

there's no coffee and the literature
is terrible, but membership is free

and numbers are up. Today, just one
other attendee, a young girl, a foot jiggler

reading a *Red Book* as worn out
as Tom's myocardium and just because

she is new here; unlike we platinum
members who bear our specters silently

she will need to speak. So, I arm myself
with easy-deploy comfort, soothing verbal

herbal tea, and believe I am ready
when she leans over to say,

You know,
there's a single
black glove lying
forgotten in every
movie theater and
a solitary bird
trapped in each
airport on earth.

And I wonder if perhaps in this waiting
life she's met more ghosts than I.

The freight elevator

The freight elevator still smells like cigarettes,
and you never know what's behind the parting
doors: sometimes it's empty, sometimes a tower

of cardboard, sometimes Larry. He's the kind
of guy who likes to get it all out there with strangers
and if you ask he'll slide in his key—of course

it's on a ring—and whisk you up to the penthouse
where all the vital organs keep the desk sitters
temperate depending on preference, season, blood

flow. Ask about the HVAC unit and the AMCO
humidifiers, just seem interested, and he'll show you
the roof and the place where the bum lived, his rags

and cans still ringing his exhaust duct nest.
If you're the right kind of guy, he may even point out
the right angles and times when the Cath-O-Lick

girls walk by below. Don't ask for a smoke
though, don't push it. Say your thanks,
shake his hand, say you'll see him again real soon.

After the double homicide

I try and compose a note
to the last remaining sister:
I'm sorry for your loss
—delete—
I know it's been a long time but
—delete—
What will you do with the baby?
After

the double homicide
I make omelet after
omelet, crack and cut
my way through
the mess. I set two places
but serve only myself.
In the unlit kitchen, steam
fills the dark. After the

double homicide I hang
Christmas lights, bunting
until numb. Grief
is an old flavor, but always
smells new: fresh
cut pine, holly, hot
plastic, turned earth
a little too close to home.

When she's away on business

I open all the windows and burn
the coffee. I quit wearing socks
and start smelling to see
what needs washed. Pigweed grows
unchecked and the garden raises bloody
poppies, bittersweet, ivy to ensnare
our foundation. Moonlight batters
the bedroom through the wood-
smoked blinds and I stop sleeping
on this lonely eggshell mattress.
The pool is turning feral.
Muskellunge prowl the cattails
and the children of the dark
neighborhood cut lupine arcs
through the whipping tallgrass,
howling at our peripheries.

I've climbed this pine to watch
the house enveloped, verdure
spilling from the trellises, wainscot,
chimney. When the hunters come
sniffing around, I know it's too late
to say the should-haves: sheers,
soap, sorry, stay. From this bole
I can see their glinting rifles,
hear their heavy tread.

Optimists always pack swim trunks

and bring their own mitts
to Yankee games. They cry
but only sometimes and only
in the shower. There are no
rainy days, simply free
car washes and new swimming
pools surfacing in basements.
Poets and long-haul truckers
are optimists deep down, so too
are most accountants and some
morticians even, but never
bartenders who know inevitability
too well.

Optimists trust their congressmen
and landlords. They worry
about lightning and sharks,
but die in subways and snowstorms
because they are lode stones
for thieves, vengeance
and drunk drivers, respectively.
The only things they leave behind
are heaps of love letters
and twenty-three years' worth
of apple stickers stuck underneath
the desk at a job that was pretty good
most days.

At the Supercuts the lonely men

At the Supercuts the lonely men
sit uneasily with their reflections,
> *Forgive me mother,*
> *it's been three months*
> *since my last touch up.*

Their plump confessors tut and pump
up chairs, drape black shrouds, cut
and listen to them bitch about losses:
taxes, football, hair. Therapy at $14.99
a pop, and it's nice to occasionally feel
the brush of a stranger's hands and not feel
guilty for staring at yourself, just for
a little while, as the past hard months
are snipped off and neatly swept away.
> *So how's it look dear?*
> *Fine, just fine, thanks.*
> *You have a good day.*

No penance, just a coupon to come on back
whenever you feel the need to unburden.

Duggers

Laying up some wood
in the middle of summer
is North Country

for thinking long term.
Sweating now to
sweat later, we toss split

logs hand to hand,
truck to cord.
Routine enough to lose

ourselves in the stacking,
we fit unique pieces
into uniform shape

like disparate soldiers
standing in formation
or uneven lovers

in the leveling bed.
But not us. It's not as if
we were square

peg round hole, but no
amount of sweating
and shifting could snug us

just too many edges
and rough corners
to ever lie flat.

The woodsmen
call them *duggers*,
logs too misshapen

to join the pile.
They're placed on top
apart from the rest

but not wasted—
they're first to burn
come winter.

Advice for a savage child

If you find   yourself alone and
quietly   hunted
                 seek water
a lake won't do   no earth-spat pond
as hide out   to lose your scent
                 the river's best
wade in   amongst the bracken ferns
crawl through   the cool sludge
                 and swim
without fear   the green snakes
do not share   poison
                 casually
kick into   the roiling shifts
ocher amber   opaque
                 with sunlight
blood rinses easily   from your hands
and paint washes   down your quick
                 brightened face
you are set free   into the wild
into the tugging   current
                 and borne
towards the sea   the looming ships
and sails   like cloudy mountains
                 lost away

Attendee training in the Butterfly Room

When I was training
to become a butterfly
wrangler, John the manager
showed me how to coax
their delicate bodies out
from the cocoon's empty husk
onto the crook
of a single finger
and toss them up
into the wet greenhouse air.

Emerged with the dawn
their bright wings fluttered
drying in the sun-warmed
trellis. Open the cages
and out they'd fly
fitful at first like a child's fingers
on new piano keys, but stronger
with each weightless beat.

But some of them
emerged broken
their stunted wings
unable to spread.
John crushed one
between thumb and pointer,
small wings dangling
like torn silk.
The weird ones he said
upset the guests.

Cleaning out the study

In a drawer full
of office refuse
I found the wrinkled
napkin note you laid
in my lunch bag

Dear husband,

and the potted palm
that I assumed
was an excellent fake
until it browned
from lack of sun and water

I'm sorry for the potato salad.

and the plastic globe
we bought in Little Burma
that omitted Australia
just a sheer stretching blue
from Vietnam to Mazatlán

I know it's not your favorite,

and in the shelving
a tiny bottle filled with sand
to remind us that even
the stones of paradise
eventually wear away

but it's all we have.

At the State Department Passport Agency

Where a harried woman explains
through bulletproof glass
why she is unable to obtain
her son's certificate of birth

from her estranged husband
because no one has seen him
for six-and-one-half years
since he went down to Oaxaca

to fish with his no-good-brother
while she watches a security guard
watch her son, resting his hand
on his pistol while her boy weaves

his wild way through the form-a-line
ropes like a slender silver minnow
threads frantically through the cañas
in silent search of shelter.

Remains

1.

All that remains are questions
from my imaginary daughter:
How quickly did you hate him?
        As soon as it was over.
What's with the letter opener?
        It suggests multiple outcomes.
When is your favorite season?
        Winter because they stack
        the scarecrows like bodies.
Why are you so hard to see?

2.

—Instructions for viewing an official lying in state—
Even dead
you may not approach
his temple body.
Sir, respectfully
remain hands-to-
pockets or better
still just keep
those fuckers
where we can see 'em.

3.

an onion
unperturbed
in a dark coffin-
like kitchen pantry
will do its domed most
to grow more onions until
the inevitable odor
of fresh green life
alerts the house
to its remains.

One little moth

trapped on an airplane
caroms skull to hat,
tail wing to cockpit

during its short
three-hundred-mile
flight and just this once

people laugh, cup
its flossy body,
let it light and pass

on towards 32A, 16B.
See the reluctance
to crush the novelty

of flight within flight
so that we fragile allies
arrive safely at the gate.

Aisle 12

is her favorite just because
it holds the smallest jars
of peanut butter. She's fond
of the feel, the snugness
of the plastic in her palm
while she watches the others,
those angelic mothers, straining
against their overflowing carts.

An ode to spectacles

I want a wiry pair
to better reflect my circumstance

little windows to my electric vagus
nerve, brawny cortices, jagged scapular
acmes

a perfect set
of setting suns, icicles rattling
in my wind
a brace of doves to grace a crooked
sinal roost

but I detect the peripheral flashes
the E
   FP
  TOZ
       the DMV quick to clear me
of charges

see the pensive remove and suasive
whirl: gesticulations out of reach

damn it if I don't get carded still
at the Squirrel Cage, stingy
librarians refuse to remove my fines

missing: one membership card
missing: one hard luck token
missing: one compliment
to a lifetime of podiums, sweaters,
cigarettes lit in spite of sideways rain.

Concerning grace

Neither the pre-
dinner request

for salvation nor
the fluid quality

of fine dancers
but the familiar

anonymity of two
old stones drug

from far afield
and set side by

side to support
the house while

the weeds grow
like children and

the untold years
wrap as heavily

as a floury apron,
a red bow tie,

a simple set
of golden bands.

3. RIVER

A Thanksgiving Letter to a Friend Stationed in Iraq

For you,

This feast: two falcons
in gyre courting
the oldest way
by chasing off crows
in the chalcedony sky
and beneath, two chairs
saddled with leaves
and soon enough snow
but poised for you
and me to sit and chat
in rounded terms
about the blue tile
in the empty kitchen
that set you weeping
for no reason, about
hollow fear and secret
locations and anger
honestly come by
or to talk weather,
hold us for a cold one
while we keep an eye
on that yew and see when
these hawks hatch.
Either way, stay hungry
or starved, whichever
feels more like home.

Yours,

When the bedroom fell

When the bedroom fell
it toppled off the house
toward the sideyard trees.
A long time coming,
it wanted for rooting
and was meanly fed
by marriage's most reluctant
conversations, weakened
during the long soak
after the miscarriage,
stiffened in exhaustion.
It kept all the pills
but no glowing reputation
for comfort, the soft
sheets packed away, shut
windows like hunger strikes
and so tonight it let go
of the foundation spilling silver
framed wedding photos, dried
nail polish, stacks of half
read novels and oxford
shirts with flapping tags out
onto the grey lawn while the rest
of the house stayed
standing: kitchen island,
basement bar, garage's traps
and useful tools. If a room
falls in a neighborhood
it doesn't make a sound
but folks will still swing by
for the yard sale.

In the cemetery walking

The hail rolls in
as the dog and I

crest a hill and pass
a hearse walking on

into the stones.
Untroubled by certainty

he trots past the fatal
limousine without looking

back. But I can't stop
thinking about myself

and being buried
in a hail storm.

And for a moment I'm sure
the hearse is stalking us

like a panther
trailing exhaust.

I start to run for the trees
when the tug of the leash

brings me back.
His nose leans into the wind

and everything is brand new
everything is right

now just like every time
I come home

because when I left this morning
he was sure this time

I wasn't coming back.
But here we are

on another walk
and when he stops

to pee on some smooth
new tomb, he never

stops to consider
his paws as they leave

two perfect prints in front
and two more close behind.

Stray

In search of approval, you may
be forgiven for wandering

away from yourself. Like a stray
in a dark neighborhood,

you're drawn to lit sills
to watch their eager faces

their hands drawing praise
to mouths like nourishment.

Do physicists hug their sons
when they use mass instead

of weight? Do strip miners smile
at daughters who top the hills

of their ant farms? How sharp
are the sheers for a black sheep?

You may not recall if he ever
showed you how to shave

or the day at the air show sitting
high as planes on cotton shoulders,

but you can still hear a leather step
scuffing up the late stairs

and cracked hands clapping
in the gymnasium swelter.

In your someday kitchen you'll pull
up from slicing a pepper and look

to the empty window wondering
what he would think of this or that.

A death in the department

On a day when the union struck over salary and its remission
the lawyers winnowing benefits abandoned the bargaining table
and word passed of a colleague's quick decline to colon cancer.
We shared it in stairwells like pennies plunked into beggar jars,

Did you hear about poor Carolyn?

And in our ill-lit lounge I found a forgotten copy of the tabular
periodic table where a photocopied hand holds the lanthanides
forever in place and I fixate on the ugly knuckles etched so clearly
in grayscale it's no wonder I quit chemistry or that the alkylating
chemo agents never stood a chance against her stubborn will to rest.

A wish for my unborn child on Christmas

We wanted a Charlie Brown
tree, some stunted little sapling
we could mother and bedeck
with lights so bright they hide
the shameful scrawny limbs.
But the frosty lots don't carry
those types of trees anymore.
They're all 8 feet tall, full and
even with names that roll off
the Boy Scouts' numb tongues
in peppermint puffs: Douglas
Fir, Eastern Cedar, Silver
Spruce. They stand straightly,
ready to be toted and twined
to the roofs of waiting SUVs.
I hope my child is a Charlie.
I hope she grows slow and
uneven, with one side all but
bare. Those trees are left
in the forest to grow their
own way, while the pretty ones
end up in my living room,
lapping water from a bowl
in desperation.

The Raquette River Club

is older than the bridge
it dangles from, and nothing lies
beneath but black ice.
The bar's crowded tonight so we take
a table at the back and stare
at the backs of heads staring
at the TV. My uncle orders two Blues
and starts ticking off the stool-sitters
one broken finger at a time.
John's wife got the cancer,
Lonny's runs a pot farm,
and Jim's has two sons by some lineman
he'd like to mow down
with his Dodge. The tired single strand
of rainbow bulbs lights the collection
of browning dollar bills
and I'd take up smoking just to fit in
but the folks at the bar had me pegged
as Downstate from go. Probably
figure I'm up for a ski with my postcard
family or a fifty-dollar dog sled ride
round Long Lake, but they don't teach you
to slalom in the flatlands and the family's
dried up. I'd buy the bar a round
if it would help the thaw, but for all the good
it'd do I think I'll just sit here
and work on this beer a bit.
And hey, would you look at that
there's a hockey game on?

Before we arrive at the party

Georgia checks her makeup in the lighted visor mirror
and, without looking away from her ministrations, lends
me some advice: *You know, instead of saying something
weird, you can just talk about sports.* At the door, the host

presses greetings into my sweaty hands and just like that
Georgia is lost to the jingling crowd of minglers. A stork
whose name escapes me as easily as Georgia enquires
if my book has found a publisher and I want to tell her

about the time I saw the Lama in Bhutan, but thinking only
of sweet Georgia say *Yeah, and it was a helluva game.* I'm free
and clear until confronted by some haunted man who just must
know about the semester and he looks down at his hands so often

I want to ask him how many ghosts he's seen, but I imagine
Georgia's frown, and so say *How about this season? Helluva season.*
I am rescued from his curious stare by Georgia who always
arrives on time and whirls me away to some waiting pair

of old puppets sitting on a settee, waving gin martinis looking
like they must have always looked, and they smile at the way
Georgia hangs from my arm and the way she leans into my wind
and the only thing I want to say is *I know, we're a helluva team.*

Transcontinental

Today I watched two strangers
fall in love on an airplane.
As I read my way through
some tattered in-flight rag,
my neighbors worked back
through each other's lives,
laughing and gasping at first
stitches and second dates,
third cousins and fourth base.
There's something about forced
proximity that pardons light
touches and long stares in the dark
mid-flight cabin. Over Delaware
he said her eyes were like
his mother's and over Idaho
she touched his rough knuckles
and then they were gone
in the deboarding shuffle.
I wonder if they were scared
apart in the suddenly bright
terminal and the crashing wash
of normalcy. I hope they held on
and shared a midnight cab
to recreate their cabin, at least
for a little longer instead of
drifting apart like so many
others who fell in love and lost
after forty thousand feet.

On Thursday night at Dominic's

After enough wine has been cleared
from the rack, I can see you

as you will be, more beautiful but greyed,

so that when you take the podium
they'll no longer think of sex;

it's faded softly to sagacity.

You laugh at some quip, pour chianti,
roll your eyes to me but can you tell

I'm no longer there? I'm sitting in that someday

auditorium, just another face watching you
work, remembering you as you were that night

at Dominic's when I finally let go.

Help Wanted

for the night shift
to welcome the tired
unsmiling dead
at the silver sliding

doors. Your inflexible
hours will provide new
arrivals with greetings
and every opportunity

to peruse our snacks
and second chances.
Duties include restocking,
minor pump repair,

executing the will
of management,
making the coffee.
Do you believe

you can do unto others?
How do you feel about Pall
Malls? Requirements:
ability to lift 40 lbs

of flesh; familiarity
with a semi-automatic;
associate's degree or requisite
experience in the fitting

and trimming of wings.
Inquire first within
yourself before applying,
laminated resumes preferred.

Float

Somewhere over Texas
my neighbor turns to me
and speaks into the dark
pressured air:

You know what? Every time I go on one of these trips
my wife picks a fight about nothing. This time she dreamed
I was cheating, so she wakes up and slaps my face. Being
six miles up I get to thinking about never coming down.

I consider letting him float
while I go home
to his bed, his wife
and the sweet sting
of her palm spreading
across my cheek
while he soars above
with his seat upright
and tray table locked
as Waco slips by below.

The ballerina's husband

Let's undress,
$\qquad$ we'll find our way down
$\qquad$ to the pond, lonely and still

$\qquad\qquad\qquad$ waiting

I'll go first
$\qquad$ wading to the hips,
$\qquad$ steady to keep the pace

$\qquad\qquad\qquad$ as dancer's do

Then you,
$\qquad$ take two steps and dive,
$\qquad$ let the water drop the melody

$\qquad\qquad\qquad$ for cricket song

The morning air
$\qquad$ passes skin to skin here
$\qquad$ where I may lift you once more, and spin

$\qquad\qquad\qquad$ to follow

Like carpet
$\qquad$ this moss welcomes rest
$\qquad$ and here amongst the stones we perform

$\qquad\qquad\qquad$ the greatest work

Touching only our feet
$\qquad$ we'll watch the sun and moon trade places
$\qquad$ and the ends and beginnings

$\qquad\qquad\qquad$ of lifetimes

Childhood's last ghazal

Never have I ever been to a funeral and not fallen apart
Never have I ever been to an airport and not fallen in love
Never have I ever run late from taking the wrong way
Never have I ever enjoyed licking up the crumbles

Never have I ever been to an airport and not fallen apart
Never have I ever drank one for the ditch
Never have I ever enjoyed watching her crumble
Never have I ever stared at your face, its port wine stain

Never have I ever drank on into the ditch
Never have I ever run late and taken the long way anyway
Never have I ever stared at your crotch, its port-wine stain
Never have I ever been to a funeral and not fallen in love

Before he deploys

bring a yearbook, white pages, cold
light beer and call up exes. Find out
who's who–married, missing you

or him or just plain missing. Go on
and cry if you want to, for old songs
and long-gone nights, but not for him.

He'll be right back, eight months
and a pay bump, come home nice
and tan. Maybe never see a thing

but sand and veils. What a thing,
hidden women. Feel free to agree
it's not ideal, but also not that different.

Deer on the golf course

How did you get here

inside 30 miles of rough

where hostas grow

I think you need to go

to play another day

on these green acres

I guess that it helps

the yards are dark

it's quiet enough now

to have another round

with no safe roads

you're drawn to places

they've killed the wolves

but soon enough we'll need

to aim at something new

Advice for the man at the bar

you should never have left her
alone

the only lily among these weeds
is sure to be sniffed by some bird
dog like me

we can pack on the charm
the moment you hit the bar,
and we'll compliment her shoes
or maybe ask her to dance like you
never do

we can take her right on back
to the last time she was in a dive
like this and she made the right
call

we'll give her just one more
chance

she'll probably say no or say
she's taken and wave us away with
that smile

but maybe not and just think
how you'll be telling all your friends
you lost her in the time it took
to order up some gin and tonics
with extra limes

At the Friday skate

the boys laid off from the rolling mill
trade insults and elbows with the Poles
and the Steamfitters 449 before retiring

to the locker room and the Goal Post
Grill to start their weekends early
because what the fuck else have they got

today but picking up kids and leaves
and disability and I thank Whomever
for the decent job and a truck that runs

and pass on a third beer, shake a few hands,
blame it on my not-so-old lady or the boss
for the morning shift and snake my way home

through the early dusk, headlights off
and pretend I'm driving the old Zamboni
laying down a clean sheet over a rough day.

The Changing Woman moves west

Water sounds—slow
rain on tent flaps,
swollen creeks
cascading—always
remind me of places.
You know

the Navajo did it best:
a place doesn't exist
until there's a story
spinning around it.
These places now,
it's all just space

—meat + no bones—
have we forgone
the sacred? How I wish
I went west with her
and made that place
a home, named it

like the Navajo
Ketl'ool: *where*
roots run deep
and placed myself
upon the dusty palms
of the Changing Woman.

Vigil

I will spend my night
on this kneeler obeisant
to my aching ACLs, contemplating

my chivalric charges: brook
no nonsense, water the flowers,
press for deliverables. When benumbed

I begin to nod, I'll hie away
to the Walmart for frankincense,
coffee, donuts for the Drive-In-Worshippers

at the Gateway to Caledonia
County Campground. On the FM
I can listen to the beech tree's epitaph

in the KZ08 traffic report,
smell the manna raining down
on the atheist's convention at the Knights

of Columbus, see the sermon
on the shelterbelt, feel each sandy
cicatrix lingering after all these thorns.

Come morning she will find me
waiting, dawn-washed and in her
raiment dazzling as a dragonfly wing

she will dub my shoulders
with her hairbrush, take off
her earrings, say what a lovely new day this is.

This is the one about going home

It starts

     with an empty bag and deciding what clothes are best for time travel

or starts

     in a snowstorm and a truck stop and *if I turned around now.*

It takes

     the last left turn and feels the old pull to plow through Gina's mailbox

or takes

     the unbuckled backseat of a midnight cab and *I think the tunnel's faster* .

It stops

     for one last cigarette and a spritz of scent under the familiar driveway pine

or stops

     at the door before the *too longs* and *too thins* under the hot kitchen lights.

It drinks

     too much with old friends to put meat on the bones of dead relationships

or drinks

     alone to ease the strangeness of hallways that seem so narrowed.

It ends

     in hasty packing and overlong hugs and suspension of disbelief

or ends

     with the high school radio station dialed in until the static finally takes over.

Topoi
or the poet's places of rest

Semi-trucks
      and secular evensong
A murder
      of crows on a windy wire
Leftover
      strawberries and their bloody bowls
Homemade
      Love Hurts tattoos
Deep beds
      or dead cities and their inhabitants
The moon
      before the scientists ruined it
Mason jars
      overflowing with loose change
Symphonies
      with a single incongruent flute
Boots
      that smell like gasoline
Empty
      bottles and other guilty secrets
Dark kitchens
      and other shrunken rooms of nonage
Kingdoms
      like poems that have no end

.

About the Author

Garrett Stack is a teacher, writer, and communication researcher based in West Michigan. Originally from Indianapolis, Indiana, he attended Indiana University in Bloomington and earned a bachelor's degree in journalism. After a very brief and unremarkable career in newspapers, he moved to Southern California to complete a master's degree in rhetoric and writing studies at San Diego State University, where he also began teaching English in the college classroom.

Penury and graduation brought him back east to Pittsburgh, Pennsylvania in pursuit of a PhD in rhetoric from Carnegie Mellon University. While there, he was fortunate to meet two fine professors, Kevin Gonzalez and Lauren Shapiro. He graduated without distinction.

Currently, he is an Assistant Professor of English at Ferris State University, where he teaches creative and technical writing, composition, and journalism. He lives 38 miles east of Lake Michigan in Rockford with his wife, Claire, and twin boys, Mac and Cully. In his spare time, he can be found playing beer league hockey, holed up in his office writing, or often napping in the yard. He has been a finalist in the Write Michigan competition, a runner-up in the Dyer-Ives Poetry Competition, and has published in a host of academic and literary journals, both in print and online. *Yeoman's Work* is his first collection of poetry.

BOOKS BY BOTTOM DOG PRESS
WORKING LIVES SERIES

Yeoman's Work: Poems, by Garrett Stack, 90 pgs, $16

APPALACHIAN WRITING SERIES

Mama's Song, by P. Shaun Neal, 238 pgs, $18
Fissures and Other Stories, by Timothy Dodd, 152 pgs, $18
Old Brown, by Craig Paulenich, 92 pgs, $16
A Wounded Snake: A Novel, by Joseph G. Anthony, 262 pgs, $18
Brown Bottle: A Novel, by Sheldon Lee Compton, 162 pgs, $18
A Small Room with Trouble on My Mind,
by Michael Henson, 164 pgs, $18
Drone String: Poems, by Sherry Cook Stanforth, 92 pgs, $16
Voices from the Appalachian Coalfields, by Mike and Ruth Yarrow,
Photos by Douglas Yarrow, 152 pgs, $17
Wanted: Good Family, by Joseph G. Anthony, 212 pgs, $18
Sky Under the Roof: Poems, by Hilda Downer, 126 pgs, $16
Green-Silver and Silent: Poems, by Marc Harshman, 90 pgs, $16
The Homegoing: A Novel, by Michael Olin-Hitt, 180 pgs, $18
She Who Is Like a Mare: Poems of Mary Breckinridge
and the Frontier Nursing Service, by Karen Kotrba, 96 pgs, $16
Smoke: Poems, by Jeanne Bryner, 96 pgs, $16
Broken Collar: A Novel, by Ron Mitchell, 234 pgs, $18
The Pattern Maker's Daughter: Poems,
by Sandee Gertz Umbach, 90 pgs, $16
The Free Farm: A Novel, by Larry Smith, 306 pgs, $18
Sinners of Sanction County: Stories,
by Charles Dodd White, 160 pgs, $17
Learning How: Stories, Yarns & Tales, by Richard Hague, $18
The Long River Home: A Novel, by Larry Smith,
230 pgs, cloth $22; paper $16
Eclipse: Stories, by Jeanne Bryner, 150 pgs, $16

APPALACHIAN WRITING SERIES ANTHOLOGIES

Unbroken Circle: Stories of Cultural Diversity in the South,
Eds. Julia Watts and Larry Smith, 194 pgs, $18
Appalachia Now: Short Stories of Contemporary Appalachia,
Eds. Charles Dodd White and Larry Smith, 178 pgs, $18
Degrees of Elevation: Short Stories of Contemporary Appalachia,
Eds. Charles Dodd White and Page Seay, 186 pgs, $18

Free Shipping.

Books by Bottom Dog Press
Harmony Series

Quilt Life, by Cindy Bosley, 108 pgs, $16
Family Portrait with Scythe, by James Owens, 114 pgs, $16
The Pears: Poems, by Larry Smith, 66 pgs, $15
Without a Plea, by Jeff Gundy, 96 pgs, $16
Taking a Walk in My Animal Hat, by Charlene Fix, 90 pgs, $16
Earnest Occupations, by Richard Hague, 200 pgs, $18
Pieces: A Composite Novel, by Mary Ann McGuigan, 250 pgs, $18
Crows in the Jukebox: Poems, by Mike James, 106 pgs, $16
Portrait of the Artist as a Bingo Worker: A Memoir,
by Lori Jakiela, 216 pgs, $18
The Thick of Thin: A Memoir, by Larry Smith, 238 pgs, $18
Cold Air Return: A Novel, by Patrick Lawrence O'Keeffe, 390 pgs, $20
Flesh and Stones: A Memoir, by Jan Shoemaker, 176 pgs, $18
Waiting to Begin: A Memoir, by Patricia O'Donnell, 166 pgs, $18
And Waking: Poems, by Kevin Casey, 80 pgs, $16
Both Shoes Off: Poems, by Jeanne Bryner, 112 pgs, $16
Abandoned Homeland: Poems, by Jeff Gundy, 96 pgs, $16
Stolen Child: A Novel, by Suzanne Kelly, 338 pgs, $18
The Canary: A Novel, by Michael Loyd Gray, 196 pgs, $18
On the Flyleaf: Poems, by Herbert Woodward Martin, 106 pgs, $16
The Harmonist at Nightfall: Poems of Indiana, by Shari Wagner, 114 pgs, $16
Painting Bridges: A Novel, by Patricia Averbach, 234 pgs, $18
Ariadne & Other Poems, by Ingrid Swanberg, 120 pgs, $16
The Search for the Reason Why: New and Selected Poems, by Tom Kryss, 192 pgs, $16
Kenneth Patchen: Rebel Poet in America, by Larry Smith,
Revised 2nd Edition, 326 pgs, Cloth $28
Selected Correspondence of Kenneth Patchen,
Edited with introduction by Allen Frost, Paper $18/ Cloth $28
Awash with Roses: Collected Love Poems of Kenneth Patchen,
Eds. Laura Smith and Larry Smith with introduction by Larry Smith, 200 pgs, $16
Breathing the West: Great Basin Poems, by Liane Ellison Norman, 96 pgs, $16
Maggot: A Novel, by Robert Flanagan, 262 pgs, $18
American Poet: A Novel, by Jeff Vande Zande, 200 pgs, $18
The Way-Back Room: Memoir of a Detroit Childhood,
by Mary Minock, 216 pgs, $18

Bottom Dog Press, Inc.

P.O. Box 425 / Huron, Ohio 44839
http://smithdocs.net

CPSIA information can be obtained
at www.ICGtesting.com
Printed in the USA
LVHW091928080720
660130LV00008B/45